FROM PILLS TO PURPOSE

DIANE BOYD

In memory of my mother.........

My mother, Brenda Boone, wrote me a detailed letter before she went on to be with the Lord. I think she knew that neither of us could bear to talk about her upcoming transition. She knew that her time was near and she left every single detail of her wishes including her insurance policy information with MetLife down to her favorite color (which we all knew was purple). I cannot find the actual letter for the life of me; however, the most important pieces are still very much present in my mind and depicted below:

"Diane, please continue to take care of the family. Watch over Mama (my grandmother) for me, Bobe (my brother), Tracy (my sister) and make sure you keep the kids in church. Diane, you were great to me, there was nothing else you could have done for me. Make sure you continue to live right so we can meet again."

Contents

Acknowledgements

Letter to my husband

Dear Babe,

Thank you for staying the course. Thank you for weathering the storms; thank you for being my strength when I didn't know I needed it; thank you for the joy, the laughter and being my peace. I could never repay you but will try my very best. I owe you my everything.

To My Father "Dada"

Thank you for your life. Though a man of few words, I thank you for always believing in me and calling me your star. I cherish and honor you as my dada. I could never repay you for spoiling me and placing the bar extremely high for anyone to follow. I love you dearly and hope I come nearly as close to making you proud as I have been to be your daughter.

Your boo-boo

To My Kids,

Kionte, Dionté, Keyona and Little Danny

Thank you for teaching me motherhood. Although I've said this to you audibly, please forgive me for being selfish along the way. Each of you have made me extremely proud to hold my title as mom. I can only wish that I've given you some seeds you can bury and they continue to take root in your lives. I love you each way beyond measure.

To My Mother Bear,

What can I say that could ever amount to what you have done for me? I love you. You inspired me to write this book. Thank you for believing in me, for pushing me and being my best friend. I hold on to the memories we created through the years and I promise to keep my promises to you.

Love,

Your baby bear

CHAPTER 1

A Child's Prayer

I can remember my mother dressing me up and putting on that itchy crimplene undergarment that I hated underneath my dresses. She would put the hot comb on the stove and you could literally smell the little bit of hair I had burning a mile away. I hated getting my hair straightened, but it had to be done. Truth is amongst all the gifts and talents God blessed me with, good hair didn't happen to be one of them. In between my hair appointments with Mrs. Buler (which I hated because she always burned me) she would straighten my hair and put those ugly pony tails all over. As a child my weeks generally consisted of Karate practice on Saturdays, piano lessons with Mr, Ronn on Saturday mornings, vocal lessons that alternated with choir practice, and singing with my dad's group. Looking back, life was awesome as a kid. We would get up early on Saturdays, my mom and dad would stop for coffee and a newspaper and we'd head through the tube for my piano lessons and my mom would always convince my dad to stop by a few yard sales on the way home. I can still smell the aroma of coffee that would linger in the car. My dad would never let me have any, he'd always say it would stunt my growth.

I liked piano lessons, Mr. Ronn was funny and he always made lessons fun and interactive. "All cows eat grass" was the bass clef; "every good boy does fine" was the treble clef. He would give me homework and my dad had purchased this old huge piano that sat in the middle of our home, which was already small and forced you to be extra cautious when walking by. Life was good; I was the youngest at home by this time. My older siblings had moved out and on their own so because of the age gap growing up I felt somewhat like an only child. My mom would tell me the story about how I was not expected and she thought I was a tumor. Truth is she truly did have a tumor, but I was there too. My mom was 36 when she got pregnant with me and she would always tell me how difficult her pregnancy was at such a late age.

She told me that after giving birth she was hospitalized for a while due to complications and my sister basically raised me. I think maybe that's why my sister and I look so much alike.

Because I was the last child at home and my mom didn't like company I learned to adapt. I had every toy you could ever imagine in my house. The front of my house looked like a toy store. I can still visualize my Barbie car, chalk board, and play house scattered about our matchbox of a living room. My cousin would jokingly tell my mom, "Your house so small you can throw a rock in and hit everybody." It really was small, but not because we couldn't afford anything bigger. In fact, my dad dreamed about having a huge home, but my mom would always say, "This is just enough room for us and, besides, I'm the only one cleaning anyways." She was right, because neither my dad nor I cleaned much of anything. She kept the house spotless. Saturday mornings consisted of the aromas of bleach, Pine-Sol, Comet, and whatever else my mom found to clean with.

My mom and her mother were very close. I looked forward to our frequent visits to London Oaks. My grandmother never learned to drive so if it wasn't in walking distance my mom would drive her. We frequented Belows local grocery store where my grandma, whom we all called Mama, would buy her groceries and pick up her society snuff. I always wondered what it was she held in her mouth all the time and why she kept a spit cup nearby; whatever it was I knew she kept it close and this was one of her pickup items anytime my mom took her grocery shopping. I loved going to London Oaks back then. Being a loner at home this was my only excitement. It was like being in a movie as a kid. I knew better than to stare or interject in their conversations, but I had my way of staying engaged without being grown so they'd call it. Most of my aunts and uncles would swing by my grandma's house and I remember being captivated by them based on what was going on that particular day. Life as I knew it was good.

CHAPTER 2

Match Made in Heaven

Looking back, my childhood was amazing and extremely busy. I think it was the last child syndrome; as unexpected as I was, my parents wanted to do everything right and make sure had a great life. All through high school I didn't get to do much, they kept a pretty tight grasp on me. I mean no outside, no football games, no nothing. I would go to my grandma's house and see my cousins getting the opportunity to do certain things and I was never granted the freedom to do so. As a kid, I was mad and couldn't wrap my head around why they were so tight on me. My dad even got me my own person phone line when I was in high school. I think he tried to accommodate for their strictness, but my mom didn't like it one bit. She never really sat me down and talked to me about her reasoning, not that she had to but it was more so do as I say and that's it. Looking back, she didn't have a reference point for it, but she just did what she felt was best for me. My mom and dad were like night and day. My mom had the ability to see right through my crap and would give me the cold shoulder as her repayment for whatever I had done or didn't do. My dad, on the other hand, his "boo-boo" (his nickname for me) could do no wrong. I honestly don't think either of them had a reference point for parenting or marriage or anything. They just did what they felt was best and figured it out along the way. The only reconciliation I can fathom is that I was so sheltered that I was just curious about life and everything in between.

I would go over my sister's house to get a sense of freedom. I was able to breathe over there. She wasn't all over my back and she just let me be. My parents didn't really like me out of their sight despite who it was, including my sister. By around 16 my dad had purchased me a cell phone. If I would get out of line or touch the tip in disobedience he would temporarily deactivate the line. This was his silent way of disciplining me. My dad was a man of very few words, but despite the fact that he didn't say much all I wanted to do was make him proud, I still do. My mom had her own way of loving me, but I did not want to hurt or disappoint "Dada" (that is what I call him). He was a humble giant who had so many talents and his voice and octave range are out of this world. He didn't say much, but when he spoke you better listen. All I ever wanted was to make him proud.

Fast forward, I met this young man. I know God knew back then that I would need him for what was ahead, but I had no idea to say the least. When I met him, I fell in love almost immediately. He invested so much into me and showed me affection and attention. This was fairly new to me, because despite the fact I was raised in what my cousins would say was a white picket fence house, growing up I rarely saw hugs and kisses or affection for that matter. So when I started to receive this things I was sold (in a good way) to the highest bidder for my love. He was just a good mixture of what I dreamed of—handsome, street smarts, intellectual and knew how to love me outwardly (get your mind out the gutter); he loved me in ways I had never seen illustrated before, and he had an intense relationship with God. I mean I read about it in school books or saw it on TV, but he showed me what I didn't see behind the walls of our small home. So the rest is history... We were inseparable from the beginning. Early on, I was still staying with my parents of course and he would come pick me up and we would go hang out and just be together. His soul was genuine and pure. I could see that he was different from the other guys and loved him some Diane. I grew up having a rep as "Oh that's so and so's sister); in fact, my sister knew this guy and raved about him from the jump. She told me he came from a great home and his family was well-to-do like ours. Unbeknownst to me, he was raised in what we considered the rich folks' neighborhood and much like my family his parents were well kept and vocally inclined as well. I remember days he'd tell me, "Diane, I want to marry you and you're going to be my wife."

I heard him, but at that time marriage was not sketched in my journey and despite how he showed me love I feared what my dad would say. I mean he had gold teeth, tattoos up his arm and despite his love for me and God I worried about how my dad would respond. We continued to date and were literally inseparable. I think from day one God knew I needed him as the pages of my life began to unfold, but I had no idea how he'd save my life at that time. For about a year and a half he consistently talked about marriage because he was a man after God's heart and I believe he knew I was made for him just as much as he was made for me. Little did I know he had lost his mom shortly before we got together and just as much as his affection was nurturing to me he needed me to help through his healing process. Sitting in the blue Lincoln that previously belonged to his mom he told me that he was going to ask my father for my hand in marriage. I agreed, subconsciously thinking he was just kidding and calling my bluff, but he was for real.

One day, after one of our typical rides in the Lincoln, he stopped at my home. Now, my mom liked him, but she would jokingly call him a hoodlum because of his gold teeth and tattoos. I think she thought it was just a phase initially but then began to realize, *Oh, this is getting serious.* My mom was pretty up front about how she felt about everything, but my dad was always quiet and didn't say much. So this particular day my boyfriend went into the house. Like always my dad was sitting in his recliner where the frame of his body had etched the impression from him sitting there so much. My boyfriend says, "Mr. Boone, I would like to ask for Diane's hand in marriage."

Staring directly at the TV, never once looking at him, my dad says, "I just got finished eating."

Wow, talk about a response. My boyfriend, stunned by the unexpected response, got up and proceeded to leave without even responding to the peculiar response almost whispered from my dad's frame. I believe I stayed there in my room while my future husband left after that awkward moment. Thinking back, I can't imagine how they must have felt on both ends.

For my boyfriend I'm sure he was thinking, *What do you mean you just got finished eating? I just asked for your daughter's hand in marriage.* My dad, as emotionless as he was, never even moved from his position, but I'm sure he thought about what was said; it was just hard to feel him out most times. So, as my boyfriend and I knew, this was not going to be easy because my dad was not going to talk about the question and my mom would shoot it down based on her own reasons.

CHAPTER 3

Dearly Beloved

"We are gathered here…" Whewwwww! I remember standing there in the living room of my boyfriend's grandmother's home and we were getting married. His grandmother knew someone who was able to officiate the wedding and here we were. Myself, my boyfriend, my father-in-law, the officiate, my boyfriend's grandmother and aunt all present and accounted for. Here we stood under the arch in her living room getting married. I was excited, nervous, and scared, all of the above. My parents weren't there because they never even wanted to discuss the subject and I recall my sister being unavailable so that was that. We said our vows; we took the covenant to love, honor and cherish, to have and to hold … until death. I remember looking in his eyes knowing I loved this man enough to do something that would change the trajectory of our lives forever. No Dad, no Mom present; all I knew was it was my wedding day and I was vowing to love this man until death did us part. I looked into his eyes as if he was the only person in the room. I recall the tears beginning to build behind the curtains of my eyes as this was monumental and I was getting married. It didn't really matter that I didn't have on a long white dress or a room full of onlookers; I was getting married.

"You may now kiss your bride…" He leaned down and kissed me. The officiator presented to the room Mr. and Mrs. Boyd. July 14 2006 changed my life and at that moment we became life partners. To have and to hold, forsaking all others.

CHAPTER 4

911, What's your emergency?

Cuddled in the bed in the wee hours of the morning the
phone rang. I knew it had to be an emergency because
who else would be calling at that time? My husband picked up
the phone irritated and half asleep. From the outside I couldn't
hear anything after "Mr. Boyd," but I knew this had to be
something important. I think I recall him saying he was on his
way shortly after the call was over. He told me his kids were
taken to the hospital after the police were called to the home
where they resided and they would be placed in the custody
of child protective services but would be at Mary View for
evaluation in the interim. By the time we got to the hospital
my mom was already there because she lived right up the street.

After getting the story behind what happened we were advised
that the process would resume and if we wished to obtain
custody we would have to go through the courts for rightful

custody. At this moment our lives changed forever. Granted, I knew the kids were a part of our lives and would always be, but I had not expected to be Mama Diane full time. Wow... Talk about married with children.

My life changed in the blink of millisecond. After countless court dates and lots of persistence we obtained full-time custody of the beautiful babies. All unique in their own way. Talk about growing up quick. Here I was, at 20, being a full time mommy. I had to figure this out quickly because there was no time to adapt. I must admit looking back I was selfish to say the least. I think I completely shut down at one point because I was forced to become someone that I had never seen before. At the time, their ages were three, six and seven. Two boys and one girl. Our lives changed so quickly that I don't think either of us saw it coming.

CHAPTER 5

Match Made in Heaven - Going through Hell

The first decade was rough. I know you're probably thinking, *Decade?* Yes decade… As selfish as I recognize my behavior now, I was so confused back then. Not confused about my love but I was a mom and a wife full time. I think everything just caught me by whirlwind. Processing my own childhood, marriage, and motherhood was rough. Don't get me wrong; I had a good childhood, but I was forced to show love and affection to these babies that needed me and I had never seen this before. Despite everything life had handed them early, they were abused, neglected, and going through transitions of, *Who is this lady we're living with?* Baby Girl was a daddy's girl by nature much like me. So now I interpret my mixed feelings of having to share my affection with someone who yearned for her father's acceptance much like me. This was one of the hardest things I had to process. My husband was an amazing father and husband. All the time I was dealing with my own demons he kept what seemed to be a straight head. Boys will be boys, so the boys didn't say much. We went through a season of bed wetting and counseling while trying to all cope with our new normal. My mother loved all the children from the very beginning. I think she quickly came to the realization that this was how things would be so her heart for kids prevailed. She had a unique bond with Baby Girl. I'm sure she saw the need for love and immediately became Grandma even before marriage. Like many grandmas, Baby Girl could do no wrong in my mother's eyes and the older she got the closer their bond grew. I depended heavily on my parents for assistance and they always stepped up to the plate. Whether it was Christmas, birthdays, hairdos, school or work; you name it, they were there.

CHAPTER 6

Boyd Party of Six

Still being a fairly new mom, my husband and I discovered we were adding an addition to our family. My pregnancy was amazing despite a few hiccups. I never experienced any morning sickness, no ankle swelling, just little two-step movements in my tummy that reminded me of new life being formed. When I discovered I was pregnant, my entire family was ecstatic; my mom was going to buy baby girl outfits and accessories every other day, my dad was my dad, my husband was excited, the kids were overjoyed, and my sister was his second mom for lack of better terms. What better support system, right? My mom; who was a cafeteria manager at the time, retired and opened up her daycare in preparation for her grandchild. Thinking back; my mom was an entrepreneur back then. It took grit and grind to wander from the familiarity of the employee to the employer. With very little experience in business she went against what she'd never seen done before and opened up Brenda's Daycare. I was ecstatic myself. Being a first time mommy with pregnancy I didn't know what to expect and couldn't think about leaving my baby in anyone else's care.

Fast forward, I found out I was having a boy and my mom jokingly said, "Oh, we putting these clothes on him." Needless to say she made exchanges and we were preparing for baby Boyd. I knew if I was having a girl her name would be Diamond Yvonne Boyd and if the sex was a boy then Daniel Collins Boyd III (DCBIII) had a nice ring to it. Just before my expected delivery date, the apartment complex we were living in discovered that there were more occupants in our apartment than the lease provided for. After asking for proof and going as far as getting records for the kids' school we weren't able to revise the lease and we were forced to find somewhere else to move. About to pop and all, we had to move and there was no way around it.

So here we go... I think I was all but eight months pregnant and having to pack up our apartment to move. God was definitely in control; we were able to quickly move into a beautiful home in a nice area. The home was nice, roomy and definitely gave me baby mansion vibes back then. Our bedroom had French doors that opened up to a balcony. The kitchen also had French doors and the patio was amazing along with a beautiful view and a yard. Pine trees overshadowed the yard and made for shady summers and not so nice yard work, but I loved it. My parents fell in love with the house and we were deemed the home for all family gatherings.

Shiny hard wood floor was all throughout the house, which was one of the things I loved about our home. And there I was on all fours rocking back and forth while contractions shot throughout my body as effortlessly. Breathing through these moments was like watching fluid drip from an IV. I was hesitant to scurry to the hospital as I had experienced a false alarm before. After about thirty minutes of what felt like agony my husband convinced me to go to the hospital. I was scheduled to deliver at Chesapeake General and the ride from

Portsmouth felt like eons. Baby Girl sat in the backseat rubbing my back as I positioned myself slightly at an angle clutching the seat belt for dear life. On the ride there my husband had already called my mom and she and my sister were en route to the hospital around 11ish on January 17, 2008.

I remember my sister and mom being present when we arrived somehow. Most importantly I kept that same angled position even after putting on the hospital gown; for some reason this gave me comfort. After receiving my epidural the rest was smooth sailing. I recall my mother and sister being there the entire time making jokes while my husband egged them on. My sister was always the videographer and captured most all the moments that you'd want as memorabilia with your first birth. On January 18, 2008 Daniel Collins Boyd III was birthed into this world healthy and full of life. While I knew I wouldn't give birth without medication I ended up having an emergency C-section because he was breech. Either way, I was glad he was here.

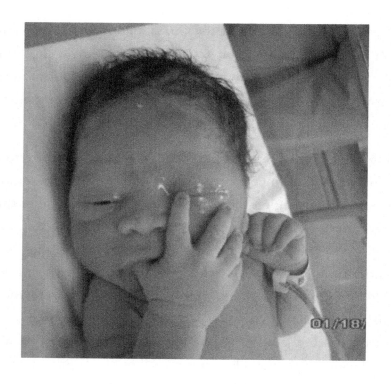

CHAPTER 7

All Roads Lead Back to Diane

Life was somewhat easy, my husband and I had an amazing support system for all the kids and daycare was my mom. We still struggled as newlyweds but we were making it work. Who could ask for anything more, right? After my mom opened her daycare, I was her daycare assistant when she needed me for any appointments she would have or as an aide to take the kids on field trips, etc. Despite the somewhat rocky relationship growing up, my mom and I became thicker than thieves. (Although I'm sure she wouldn't like that phrase.) My mom was always my rock whether my husband and I needed help with the kids, a bill or to mediate our marital spats. lol. She was there; because I never had many friends I would tell my mom everything. Wrong idea. I would get over it and she'd still be mad, but that's what moms do.

I can't recall the exact day (I'm sure he husband would remember the year, he remembers everything by year) I was watching the kids for my mom because she had a doctor's appointment. She always trusted me watching the kids because she knew I would really watch them considering the backlash that comes along with a daycare child getting hurt. I was literally her assistant. This particular day was different though. For a little over a month or so my mom had a pretty persistent cough, which sometimes interrupted or prevented her ability to sleep at night. She would go to her doctor or ER from what I can remember and they'd tell her it was a typical cough from a cold I assume and they'd prescribe her the codeine to aid with sleep at night, but it was only temporary and I think after a time my mom knew there was more to it. This day I was watching the kids and we had made our way up to the porch as I knew she was about to pull up. The kids would light up like Christmas trees when they saw her coming because she had a genuine love for all the kids in Brenda's Daycare. This day she pulled up with lunch for the kids but her eyes looked pained. She sat down in the porch chair and instantly started to cry.

"What's wrong, Ma?" I asked.

She replied, "The doctor said that I have to be on oxygen as my oxygen levels are low."

I said, "Oh Ma, this is only temporary, this is going to help you and God will heal you, watch." I think I provided slight comfort in her moment of distress. I think even the kids sensed her sorrow because we all sat there mute.

Shortly after, the oxygen van pulled in front of the driveway and began to unload the small bottles of backpack oxygen. My nephew was there to help take them into the house. I recall the oxygen man showing us how to assemble the oxygen and tubing before he disappeared down the street. I think we were all still in disarray but we literally were stuck in that moment. That moment changed my mother's life forever.

She hated wearing that oxygen and although she was prescribed to keep it on nonstop she would pretend there were times when she didn't need it. She battled with this being her new normal and we both continued to pray for complete healing, but the reality was she still needed to wear the oxygen. At that very moment it was like I transitioned from her daughter to her prayer partner, her cheerleader, her coach, her nurse, her friend, her everything, next to God of course. Through it all she still reverenced God and believed in her healing one day.

For her 62nd birthday I recall planning a huge surprise where I invited all her friends, family far and in between to come celebrate her. Each brought gifts that signified what she meant to each of us. I mean we had a DJ, grill, and food galore. I remember wanting her to feel loved beyond measure that day. Her favorite color was lavender so anything I could put my hands on to make her smile and was within my reach was hers. Everyone assembled at my sister's house and I rode with her in the van making sure she had her oxygen and water nearby. Even with oxygen she had a really bad cough so we kept mints and bottled water on hand to soothe her throat.

She had an amazing time, but I had studied my mom like clockwork. I had it down to a science when she was winded, tired, holding back a cough, struggling to breathe or merely struggling not to break down. I think I knew her better than I knew myself. Suddenly, my life was no longer my own; my sole purpose was ensuring that my mother bear had what she needed in any capacity. That was my job. For a while I lost sight of everything. My husband can attest I literally only saw my mother and her needs. Those were our nicknames for each other. She was my mother bear and I was her baby bear. The pictures below are from her birthday party.

Honestly I don't know how we started calling each other that, I think we got the concept from the mama bear story. It was our language and we understood each other clearly. We would chuckle because we had little phrases that only we knew and I think that gave us comfort during uncomfortable situations. Well, the birthday party was a huge success; after she opened up gifts and chatted for a while I think we made up an excuse for her to leave because I could tell she needed her oxygen and it was time to go.

Despite her inability to breathe most times as her condition progressed, she still kept her daycare open. At the onset of her condition, diagnosed as pulmonary fibrosis, I obtained FMLA through my employer, which allowed me the flexibility of being at her beck and call. Simple tasks became extremely difficult for her, but her passion for kids persevered and we kept the daycare open longer than we expected. I remember there would be days when parents would come for pickup and she'd take her oxygen off because she didn't want them to know what was going on. Hopefully the parents wouldn't talk too long or the child wouldn't go haywire because she couldn't last long without her oxygen. Watching my mother literally deteriorate before my eyes was one of the worst things mentally I've ever had to deal with.

CHAPTER 8

Refill

Eventually, even with my help, the daycare was more than we both could handle. We had a system, but as her health declined she couldn't risk taking off her oxygen for the sake of a parent pickup. Sadly, we closed Brenda's Daycare. God knew the timing was right, though, because some of the kids moved and our decision to shut down business was put into perspective. The parents were still never notified of my mother's health condition and the way God worked things out we didn't have to disclose it. Taking a quick trip back down memory lane, I always suffered with RA (rheumatoid arthritis) even as a child, but I believe stress levels and problems in life heightened the existing issue. I never complained, though, because the issue at hand was my mother and she needed me. My marriage was suffering because I couldn't find a balance and my life was consumed with my mother. She needed me this seemed to be the right thing to do at the time. I was her sole caregiver. I remember days going to my parents' house before work to help her use the restroom or take her something to eat. Although she had a nurse she wouldn't take a bath, use the restroom or really anything without me. We had a rhythm of how we did things. I knew she got out of breath easily so doctors' visits sometimes required her to have oxygen in her nose and mouth. Not recommended of course, but I did what I needed to do so she knew I was fighting with her. I would tell her often, "We're in this together." She worried about worrying me, and I was worried but I couldn't let her see that. As far as she knew I was Super Woman. But at night Super Woman cried, in her car she cried out to God. I gotta admit I became angry. I had other siblings but somehow she only wanted her baby bear. I mean we were like Thelma and Louise; I was the ying to her yang; somehow I think we became each other's safe haven.

She had started to sleep in the back room that used to house small kids running around, wiping their hands everywhere and screaming the alphabet. This was not her bedroom. Her little back pack oxygen was no longer sufficient for her oxygen needs and she had progressed to the machine with the filter. Aside from periodic doctors' visits and random visits to church on Sunday, for which she had enough energy to dress herself, she didn't do much moving around. She moved to the back room where she slept because the oxygen tank was loud and she didn't want to disturb my dad because he now became the sole bread winner and was still working. In the back room I was able to maneuver around as needed to help her without distraction. We kept the daycare decor up for a while. I think it gave her a sense of endearment and hope.

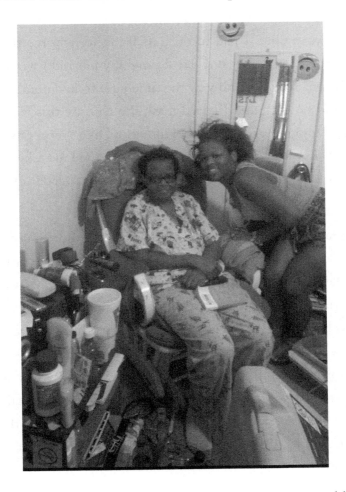

I recall one day going to my car and calling my siblings screaming, "I need help; I can't do this alone." Although I wanted help, I knew that, as much as my siblings loved our mother, I had been assigned for the job.

How was I supposed to deal with this? Who was supposed to be there for me like I was there for my mother? My husband couldn't register what was going on and my life as I knew it was a whirlwind. I had to do something to help me through this pain. I remember one day leaving my job and I would pop two tramadols. Generally by the time I got to my mom's house, I would be high and I could mask the pain by this feeling of temporary euphoria. My initial intention, like everybody else's, was, *This is just something for right now.* It helped me take care of my mom and block out the reality that she was declining right before my eyes.

I appeared strong to her; she would tell me she didn't know how I did it, but I knew it was an escape method. The pills I used to take as prescribed had now become my escape mechanism. Eventually it became pills to get up in the morning and pills to go to bed at night. What started off as two pills maybe every four hours now progressed to three, four or five pills in a setting. My tolerance was high because of the abuse and I was taking more pills than I had a prescription for. Between hospital stays with my mom, still trying to balance my marriage by a thread, and ER visits, this was the only thing I felt helped me cope.

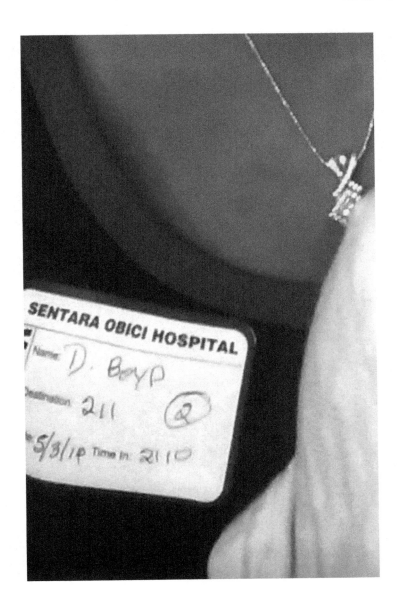

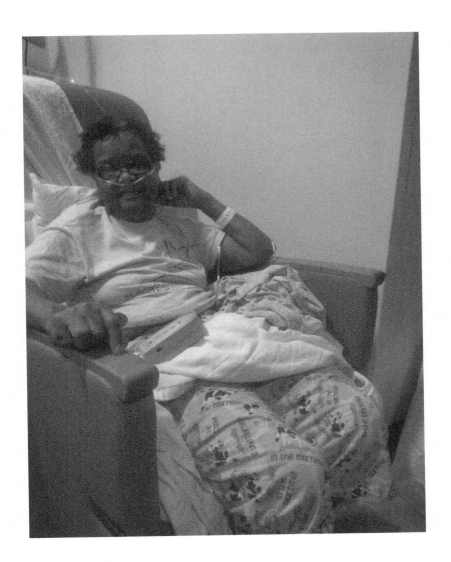

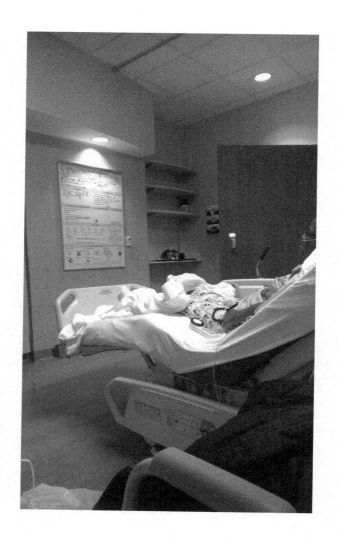

CHAPTER 9

High Maintenance

Most days I would wake up counting my pills to see how many days I could last before trying to figure out what to do next. A fresh bottle made me feel empowered, although I knew 60 pills wouldn't last long at the rate I was going. I remember days when I would lie across my mother's bed being sick as a dog because of withdrawals and because of overuse of my prescriptions they weren't lasting me long at all. Withdrawals were the worst, mine included brain zaps, diarrhea, mental fog, fatigue, lack of appetite, and restless leg syndrome. It feels like someone rings your body like a wash cloth but never straightened you out. I was fighting a silent battle that nobody around knew anything about. How in the hell did I end up here? I was my father's baby girl, the one that sang in the choir, yet here I was addicted to pills. How did this happen to me? During the downward slopes I tossed these thoughts through my mind.

However, as soon as the phone rang with an automated message from Walgreens saying that my prescription was ready I quickly forgot about my quarrels. My reasoning was who else was going to do it? I mean it was this or what? Little did I know God kept me in His hands. In between refills I would take some of my mom's codeine cough syrup. It wasn't the same, but it helped ease the body chills and aches just a little.

CHAPTER 10

01.23.15

I was spiraling out of control, I had lost myself, but one thing was constant—I was making sure my mom was okay. I wondered how my family or siblings didn't notice that I was changing right before their eyes. I don't know, maybe we were all in a disarray because of the situation at hand, but I knew I wasn't myself. I had gotten down to 129 lbs. soaking wet and I was literally skin and bones. I look back at pictures and I relive the emotions in my eyes. I know exactly which pictures were taken when I was high and in which pictures I was going through withdrawals. The hospital bed had become my permanent bedding and I was okay with that. I slept there and most visits Baby Girl was by my side, she was never too far behind. We were rocking it out with her my mom no matter what.

I recall her last hospital visit just like it was yesterday. It was different though. I knew my mom was tired and that day she called me at work and told me she thought she needed to go to the hospital. Of course, I left immediately as I always did and went to pick her up. I prepared her two tanks as I usually did just in case she needed to put one in her mouth. I just would look at her and wonder, *Why my mom?* I wanted to trade places with her so bad; she didn't deserve this. She was one of the good guys, she never smoked or drank or partied or anything for that matter. I got angry with God because I had some recommendations for who may have been ready before her, but who was I to choose? I beat myself up questioning why and literally watching the person who gave birth to me dwindling away, and there was nothing I could do about it. Needless to say we checked into the ER and they took her immediately to the back due to her inability to breathe. I would pull up front, lift her out and then go move the car while Baby Girl would go in with her. She loved Baby Girl. She was her sidekick and by being there so much she even knew how to operate the oxygen gauges and help her as needed when I wasn't close by.

So we checked in and after their normal routine they told us she would be admitted and transported to the main hospital. I was okay with this; I felt like she would get all the oxygen she needed and hopefully get better, but something about this visit felt different. Routinely I'd call my dad and siblings to keep them posted. They felt a sense of assurance knowing Baby Girl and I were there and she was in good hands. Just like any other visit doctors were in and out. I remember a tall Arab doctor coming in to introduce himself. He stood not too far from the door and proceeded to go over the latest test results. He shared something that we hadn't heard quite like he put it before. I remember him standing there telling us that basically my mom wasn't expected to last long. Her lungs were in an extremely bad condition, which was why her breathing was worse. He stood there emotionless and rendered this verdict as if he was God. He showed no mercy that this may make her give up hope or that any fight she had could be thrown out the window. He said we could decide to put her on life support to make her comfortable but if not she'd need to be on bipap machine at night. I knew at that very moment she was going to let go and let God have His way. He finished his statement and told us to let him know if we had any questions and he just left. I was angry at him for a while; I felt like as a doctor he should have talked to me first then let me decide whether that was something she needed to hear. Shortly after, the chaplain began to come in and talk to us periodically, both of us together and separately. My mom expressed her worries about leaving me and I expressed my frustration that she was fading right before my eyes. I think my mom knew that something was going on with me. Maybe she didn't know what, but she knew that I was different.

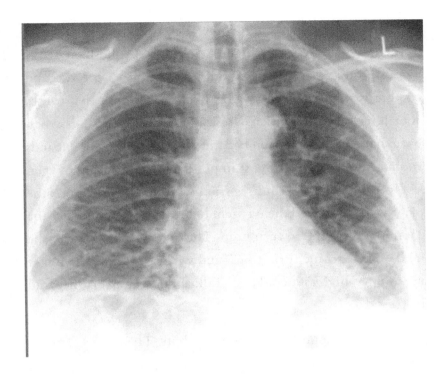

I think I recall the doctor leaving and my mom looking lost. I remember telling her the doctor didn't have the last say so and we were still waiting on God. In the back of my mind a little piece of me lost hope too. At that moment she said that she didn't want to be resuscitated and if something happen it was God's will and she didn't want them pumping on her chest.

The morning of January 23, 2015 I remember her waking me up a number of times that morning to go to the bathroom. I found it strange that she had to use the bathroom so much, but of course I didn't say anything. After around the fourth time me helping her, the last time the nurses put a bed pan under her so she wouldn't have to get up as movement had become very difficult for her. I remember her being on 15 liters of oxygen, which was the highest amount the hospital tanks would produce, and she was still struggling to breathe and gasping for air. Pulmonary fibrosis is a condition that causes your lung tissue to harden. Typically the lung expands when we exhale, but if the tissue becomes hard it no longer expands and makes for painful almost impossible breathing and oxygen levels. I remember the nurses tried to see if she could breathe okay as they lowered the oxygen, but the moment they left the room she'd tell me to turn it up. The last time on that day she said, "Diane, come turn it up," and when I checked the meter it was up as high as it could go. Talk about feeling crushed and helpless.

Her last few minutes still seem like a blur. The nurses came in and she asked them to remove the bed pan. I remember walking out to use the hallway bathroom. The nurses were negotiating with her why they couldn't remove it and I remember Baby Girl running down the hallway a few minutes later screaming and crying, saying she was gone. The nurses closed the door and began to unhook the tubes, and the oxygen, and every other piece of equipment she was connected to. They took the bed pan and fixed her clothing and pulled the white sheet up to her chest. I remember Baby Girl and I sitting there in silence. I began to kiss my mom and rub on her arms telling her how much I loved her. I'm sure she knew it, but it just felt right. She looked so peaceful; though it sounds cliché she looked sound asleep.

My siblings and father had already been called when I saw her condition worsening. At this time they were already in transit to the hospital. I remember my brother asking me, "What's wrong, Diane? Mama alright?"

I replied, "Yes, just get to the hospital as soon as you can."

I can't recall the order in which my siblings arrived but I remember being numb. I don't recall crying at all. This wasn't a time to cry. I think my tears just wouldn't fall. I had to be there for my sister and brother. Who else was? I remember my sister walking in and throwing her gloves on the floor once she realized she was gone. My brother said he'd give anything to have her back. Though our sorrow filled the room, my mother's spirit was free. Only a shell was present, but her spirit was free. Shortly after, my grandmother, uncle and his wife walked in and sat down. It wasn't until I announced that she was gone that they realized she wasn't sleeping. It crushed me to see my grandmother break down. My grandmother and my mother were extremely close. For so long my mother masked the seriousness of her condition to her family in fear of them worrying about her.

Suddenly, my dad walks through the door. Yet again he asks if she's asleep. "No, she's gone," I replied.

He never shed a tear. He immediately said, "Let us pray."

I was startled, "What do you mean pray? Right now, you're not going to cry or fall out or scream?" I just remember staring at the vessel I knew as my mother thinking, *What happens now?*

I vaguely recall putting her dentures in so I could gather a few pictures before they took her away. At that moment, a piece of me left with her. In fact, I think a piece of every one in that room left with her when she transcended to Heaven. My brother and sisters and I waited around until the funeral home came to pick her up. I remember us sitting in the lounge area staring at one another in a daze. We were all still in shock and disbelief and I don't think it really hit us that she was gone. At this particular time my husband was away on work in Japan. After receiving the news, he planned to travel back to Virginia as we prepared to lay my mother to rest. I must apologize; everything after that point seems like a blur.

I stayed high enough to numb the pain while trying to figure out how was I going to get more pills as the high would go down. I remember spending several nights out at the cemetery. I would park my car and just sit out there. It was pretty quiet to say the least. Every time I would think about leaving or walking to my car I'd hear her say, "Diane, what time you coming back?" or "Why you gotta leave, Diane Boone?" (This is what she'd say when she was alive.) There was even one night I got a blanket and put over the dirt because I swore I could hear her saying she was cold. I'm sure you're thinking I was losing my mind. This is true and I couldn't agree with you more.

CHAPTER 11

Gamble

I'd gotten pretty familiar with all different ways I could try to get more meds when I'd run out. The lies ranged anywhere from I was going out of town and the location where I was going didn't have a Walgreen pharmacy to my pain had increased and the doctor needed to change my pill count. Sometimes they'd give me five pills until they got clearance from my doctor. Five pills ... what was I going do with five pills? I had gotten to the point of taking that many in one setting. Once your tolerance gets that high, even if you try to take two or three you could still experience withdrawal symptoms. It was a constant mental, physical, and emotional agony.

Shortly after my mom passed my car was repossessed. I know I had fallen behind on the payments but I felt like I could eventually get caught up. The light bill was behind and the lights turned off because they had disconnected them, but "Grease Monkey" from around my old neighborhood knew how to turn them back on for a few dollars. I was literally living in hell. Every day coming home in fear that they had disconnected the lights and put a lock on the box was devastating and stressful and I didn't have the nerve to tell my husband. My dad let me use his car until I figured something out so I was just barely keeping my head above the water. My marriage was holding on by a thread because I couldn't tell my husband I was addicted to pills and losing my mind. The world as I knew it was crumbling right before my eyes. I had been laid off work the day after my mom passed so at this point I was living off unemployment. This was roughly 300 weekly, which was a smack in the face. I had hit rock bottom and I couldn't figure out how to get out of this black hole.

Pretty soon my lies for refills were being rejected and I was running out of options. I ran across someone who had access to pain medicine and would sell them to me for about $20 a pill. Literally, my entire week check was going toward pills or almost all if not the entire amount because you never want to run out. They rarely got the pills I was used to getting and they didn't last as long, but to avoid being sick you will take what you can get. So here I was buying pills. Like there were days when I would feel like a complete fool but I still did it. I was taking money out of my husband's and my joint account and sometimes even overdrawing the account. I was in too deep. I remember days when he would walk in the house after discovering I had overdrawn the account and he would be furious. Most days I was either sick or too ill to really receive what he was saying, but God never let him leave me when he had every right to. I went from tramadol to hydrocodeine, to morphine in pill form, even Percocet if only they were available. I would tell myself, *I can stop if I want,* but who was I fooling? This monkey was riding my back and had no intentions of getting off. In fact, I can remember some nights dozing behind the wheel and coming to just in time enough to avoid an accident, I had it bad.

I'd been taking pills consistently for about six years, but the abuse went on for about four years total. I remember one night calling my contact to see if they had any pills or something because I was sick. I remember very vividly that they talked cold crap to me on the phone like never before. In my mind I thought, *How dare you talk to me like that?* almost as if I was a fein. I mean I had fallen into a sunken place this deep where you'd allow somebody to talk to you any kind of way. At that moment, I remember hanging up the phone mid conversation, blocking their number and at that moment in the car I asked God to take it all away. I said, "God, this is bigger than me and is a stronghold in my life. I need you to take it away." Can I tell you I never looked back from that moment? Generally I would endure sickness from withdrawals; at that moment God did it and I owe my life to him. He literally took the urge away, the ill feeling away,; He took that burden from me never to return. God is just waiting for us to tag Him in. The entire time He never let me sink until death, yet He let me go through so that someone else wouldn't have to endure what I went through. I'm thankful to Him and I owe Him my all. I'm a witness that when you're ready to surrender He will bear your cross so that you don't have to go through to get to. He just wants you to tag Him in. Needless to say, that wasn't the end of my battle. I wish I could lie to you, but the intent of this story is to be transparent and heal. I recovered from pill addiction, but how many of you know that the enemy doesn't have any new tricks? He still uses old ones.

CHAPTER 12

Blurry Nights

So I recovered from my pill addiction, I shook that demon and felt really accomplished. But I only replaced the pills with alcohol, cognac to be exact. That was my drink of preference. I mean I was drinking daily, all day or to the point where I was consuming large amounts daily. I had an insane tolerance level for alcohol and would literally drink just about anybody under the table. So embarrassing, but that was my truth. After several come to Jesus meetings and telling myself I wouldn't drink again, the next day I would go right back. Boy the enemy said, "If I can't get you one way I'll try another way."

People always talk about generational curses; well, I believe this to be true and I'll explain why. My mom's mom was addicted to snuff (society) and my mom picked that trait up. A host of family drug abuse, alcoholism, you name it, the hard stuff.

I had succumbed to one of the strongholds that kept many in my family bound. I had to get out of this rut and quickly because it was wearing on me. I had gained over 20 pounds from drinking every day and I prayed for my liver daily, but that didn't stop me from taking the first sip. I mean I knew the price of the bottle down to the T. Enough was truly enough...

The same exact way that I kicked my pill addiction I remember going to God the same way. I got tired of waking up to a hangover, not living according to God's will for my life while literally losing everything. I remember saying, "God, take the alcohol addiction away," just like that, and I'm thankful for Him not giving up on me when I know I probably would have. God knew that I had so many gifts that I hadn't even tapped into and thankfully He didn't allow pills or alcohol to be the cause of my nonexistence. See just like many of you I struggled with writing this book or telling my truth. I feared what people would think or how they would view me. But thank God for delivering me from people because they don't have a Heaven or Hell to put me in. And whether or not you wish to believe it this book is ministering to someone right now who doesn't know their way out.

See the thing is it's the people who look like you and me who are silently fighting a battle that you know nothing about. I've come in contact with beautiful ladies who battle this addiction and it's resulted in many of the struggles I've outlined above. They cry silently at night from withdrawals trying to figure out how to get more pills and get out of this tug of war. Then, if you're still newbie in your addiction, you may say you don't have a problem and you can stop wherever you wish. Oh okay ... I've heard it all before.

I'm so thankful that I came out of that battle. I mean I felt like both substances empowered me to do anything I put my mind too—clean a house, wash my car, all the things I felt would otherwise wear me out or take too long. How many of you can attest that you can do ALL things through Christ? He saved me and I solely depend on Him. Fast forward, I'm 34 and living my best life and thankful to be writing this book to minister to someone going through this same struggles. God is a keeper and He will bring you out of anything, if you first confess with your mouth that you have a problem and seek help. I'm so thankful that I never once had to step foot in a rehabilitation center, but instead I was counseled by the master doctor, Doctor Jesus, and He took away my illness instantly after I turned it over to Him.

My story could have ended very differently; someone else could have tried to depict the story on my behalf because of my poor decisions resulting in my demise. I'm thankful for a changed mind and the desire to do better. My goal is to reach back and help so many others who are able to relate to any of the strongholds that I have mentioned above. I'm creating a help group where we encourage each other and send out weekly encouragement to poke you and provoke you to new beginnings. Your victory is right on the other side of your fear and you must take action to overcome and conquer what wants to keep you down. This does not have to be how your story ends; in fact, I'd like to partner with you and be your personal accountability partner as you reach your breakthrough. Your breakthrough doesn't necessarily have to be a pill addiction, but addiction, no matter the form, is still a stronghold and if not handled with the help of God will leave you feeling helpless and dependent on whatever that thing is. I provoke you to first forgive yourself, ask God into your heart, and start your road to recovery. I pray this book changes your way of thinking, lets you know that you are not alone, and, most importantly, provokes you into believing that if I can change and come back to save others, there are also others depending on you defeating this stronghold so that you can come back and throw out the life jackets. Will you take the first step? Say this prayer with me:

Heavenly Father, I come to you thanking you for life. Lord, I ask that you come into my heart and forgive me for my sins. Father, I'm sorry for not loving myself as you have loved me and died for my sins. I thank you for giving your life so that I can have the right to Life and in abundance. Please wash me clean with your blood and give me the power daily to overcome whatever the stronghold is that is acting as a distraction. I know that you hold all power in your hands and this stronghold is nothing compared to the power that you hold. Lord, I thank you in advance for restoring what the enemy thought would defeat me; in fact you have raised me just like you did on the third day of your resurrection. I will submit to you daily and lean not unto my own understanding. I love you and seal this prayer with Amen and it is SO! Always Remember, there is life and purpose after trauma.

Made in the USA
Middletown, DE
08 July 2021

43819624R00046